wowers

Previous collections Paul Groves

Academe
Ménage à Trois
Eros and Thanatos

# PAUL GROVES

## wowsers

seren

Seren is the book imprint of
Poetry Wales Press Ltd
Nolton Street, Bridgend, Wales
*www.seren-books.com*

The right of Paul Groves to be identified as the
Author of this Work has been asserted in accordance with
the Copyright, Designs and Patents Act, 1988.

ISBN 1-85411-307-0

A CIP record for this title is available from the British Library.

The publisher acknowledges the financial assistance
of the Arts Council of Wales.

Printed by Bell and Bain, Glasgow.

Cover photograph: Jeff Carter, Tobacco Road, Ovens Valley

# Contents

# At Partrishow in the Black Mountains

The sun rises over England, and sets over Wales.
We look eastwards for each new dawn, westwards
for every sunset. There is fresh blood at dusk.
It is a wonder the hills don't redden with it, the streams
run like urgent haemorrhages, clotting behind boulders,
coagulating among rock pools. The air also is unstable,
thick with invading words. Century by century
the English tongue has licked or lashed
the Welsh identity. Spin the dial of your radio:
London is here, dominant in this quiet valley
where the saint was murdered. His church
is wedded to the hillside with a ring of silence.
Its stones are those laid with effort and precision
a thousand years ago. The builders, among these trees,
these hollows, had the faces and hands of men,
                                        but the vision
of angels. Turn the radio off. Quietude returns.
Or let it play, night and day, raucous and foreign;
within a week it will have succumbed, its batteries
                                        drained.
But the stream will still be here, as will the church.
The faith will remain. The hope might even strengthen.

# Rudolf Hess at White Castle, Monmouthshire

Imprisoned at Maindiff Court, Abergavenny,
he has an afternoon's parole – with two guards.
He has visited this battered edifice before
and asked to return.
                    It is quiet summer,
somnolent as Lüneburg Heath.
                          That brooding skyline
resembles the Harz.
                  He nods, askance.
"The Black Mountains," says one of the bored tommies.
He watches a bee invade pendulous purple petals.
Does he know that, although this plant is poisonous,
digitalis can treat an ailing heart?
He eyes the flanking towers for the last time.
Sheep graze as they have for centuries.
                             He sighs.
War is such a waste.
                  Returning in the camouflaged truck,
they stop for a drink.
                  It is not against orders.
He signs a beer mat, now in the town museum.
The ruins are solitary under the Welsh sky,
surrounded by silent countryside.
                          The bee
visits another bloom.
                  His heart aches
for childhood, for those times before farce
took over.
              A butterfly alights on a red clover.
Strange how the wings of a fritillary
are speckled like the inside of a foxglove.

# To the Tenant Farmer with the Lee-Enfield Rifle

I am the grandson you never knew, born six years
after your death to your eldest daughter
and a son-in-law you were unable to meet.
Do not blame yourself. Thousands commit suicide
every year, and a gun is as good a way as any
to cancel thought. It took over half a century
for the silence to break, for me to be told
the unpalatable truth. Strangely, I find it palatable.
I want to shake you by the hand. It demands
a certain kind of courage to do what you did then,
in the kitchen or an outhouse or sitting on the stairs
– your daughters even now will not say which.
But listen: Hitler lost, and Mussolini also
got his comeuppance. The war dragged on
for four more years, yet the world that followed
managed such mass-produced newness as almost
takes the breath away. Perhaps we could
talk about Glenn Miller and Leslie Howard,
how they fell from the air into pure conundrum;
and Max Miller, The Cheeky Chappie; and
you should know that *White Christmas* was a hit
the next year, as were *This is the Army, Mr. Jones*
and *We'll meet again*. Will we, having never
met in the first place? You are a part of me;
your genes are crucial to the mystery
of my personality. But my gun is lighter.
It takes only small black cartridges of ink.

# Bequest

The cracked mirror gave him a harelip. He zipped up
and turned. The cistern laughed at us. Brotherly love!
Twenty years in Canada and he wants an equal cut.
"You won't get away with it," I said. Back in the office
the solicitor cleared his throat to read. The prodigal
relaxed on a hard chair. Wives gripped handbags,
a white-water ride. Had the old girl had a deathbed
change of heart? Maureen consoled me in the car park
later. The fatted calf had been killed after all.
I hold out ten-year-old hands to a seven-year-old brother,
his face ashen above the smashed ice of a pond.
With commendable foresight I loosen my grip.

# So Now You Know

Rivington Service Station. The first of October.
And delegates returning from the Labour Party Conference
in Blackpool. An official Rover. A minder-cum-chauffeur;
a male secretary; a cabinet minister. Business-suited
though not spivvy in dark glasses, they entered
for refreshment and were hardly recognised –
to my amazement. I wanted to tap shoulders
and urgently whisper: 'Look who that is!' Later
I was in the men's room and saw the chauffeur
standing around eyeing a cubicle door like a faithful dog
anticipating the reappearance of its owner.
Dutifully, the master exited – having activated the flush –
and washed his hands beneath one warm sprinkler tap.
I was drawn into occupying the cubicle next.
I slid the bolt across. A warm farmyard smell; and there,
bobbing innocently, the unsluiced turd.
This guy could be prime minister before I'm drawing
my pension. He's brilliant, a master of diplomacy
and prevarication, honed statement and smiling
half-truth. I could imagine some sad groupie fishing out
the ordure for posterity, to be preserved chemically
in a vacuum flask labelled with place, date, and maker
so grandchildren could gape in awe decades hence
or a friend giggle incredulously a good deal sooner.
Elvis's sweat-stained handkerchief, December 1975.
Ringo's dog-end, June 1963. No, it was never a temptation.
It was briefly fascinating then quickly repulsive.
I disposed of it as if it were an injured snake,
sending it along plutonian passageways
under the car park to the main sewer.
I saw him on television the following night.
I smiled darkly, hoarding my secret.

# When Paul McCartney Stayed

Cousin Madge was eating bread and jam
at teatime when a black Mercedes drew
up beside her gate. A famous name
    got out of it, and threw

caution to the wind by taking off
his Raybans. The astonishment was total:
she clutched her temples, for the bulletproof
    car had brought a Beatle

to her Walsall semi. When he pressed
the doorbell, she advanced with overflowing
eagerness to answer it. He said:
    "Hello there, how're you doing?"

Time shrank to nothing. All her tight resolve
    lay useless as a cinder.
The world refused, that minute, to revolve
    as down the path strode Linda,

the singer's wife. Cousin Madge could cope.
Her invitation was assured: "Come in!"
Soon she'd cut some cake, and a best cup
    rose past the well-known chin.

They talked till late. When everything was said
she showed them to their unassuming room:
three plaster ducks, a creaky double bed.
    Linda's ritzy perfume

provided a strange counterpoint. Madge felt
strong as Atlas, wise as Aristotle.
She blurted, "If you want, give me a shout
    for a hot-water bottle."

The home help entered with her master key
next morning. Madge's eyes were bright as flame.
She'd curled up in a corner. Presently
        two paramedics came.

# Visit to Virginia

I remember her entering from the orchard
with those empty round eyes, behind which lay no evil
and only occasional madness. The trug contained
crab apples, spindle tree seeds, whitebeam berries,
a collection which matched her strange ambivalence.
We talked about childhood holidays at St Ives,
her Hyde Park Gate home, and the house – so full of life –
at Brunswick Square. She made me tea.
"My husband helped govern the Singhalese, and this
is from their country." I nodded, impressed, half-
remembering Leonard's seven years in the Colonial Service.

"Are those for dyspepsia?" I gestured towards the tablets
she cradled in her palm. "Headaches. They help me think."
She had said the previous day how, during her first attacks,
birds had spoken in Greek, and Edward VII had cowered
in her garden, whispering obscenities.
"Don't worry," I'd said, "the old fool
has visited mine too, dripping innuendo like a tap
in a seraglio." She had not believed me. I lowered
another sugar cube into my cup, so that the warm liquid
rose through it, tainting its crystalline whiteness.
She pointed at the Millais *Ophelia* above the chaise longue:

"Sometimes I fancy that is me."
I should have frowned, muttered 'Nonsense', and said
how healthy she looked. But she was pale from overwork
and the shadows of London. "Here in Sussex
I soon recover," she stated. "After lunch let us walk
down by the river. The Ouse is so graceful,
like a lifeline, an eternity, a challenge, an invitation,
a strong mother, an errant guest, a City banker in dark clothes
saying it is too late and that I must return to a nobler past
or to a future which has palpably fewer terrors."
"Yes," I replied, "I should like that very much."

# Wish You Were Here

Your arms are raised to bring the washing in.
Beyond you the sun sets over Limburg.
This is the German miracle: that it is possible
to keep whites white in the air of the Ruhr...
hence perhaps your comical grimace.
But you insist you're the better-off sibling,
the one with the depreciation-proof Merc.
Diana, you old huntress, tracking down
a well-heeled industrialist and wounding him
with Cupid's arrow, you loved the lifestyle
well before you experienced it; you fell for
the idea of Europe, the stainless steel, the autobahnen
where fear alone limits the driver's speed.
I call you Frau D. If only you knew.
My angst is personal, very British; I am
the wunderkind who never made it to
*Übermensch*. So go ahead, unpeg
your husband's suspect shirts; check them for grime;
and write to say you're having a good time.

# Protector

Police and paramedics know the score:
cars smashed almost out of recognition
along the motorway. Hank of hair.
Solo finger. Blood and piss and bone.
Stench of oil. Sometimes someone screaming
with unearthly vigour. They will say
that after the injections, the foaming
of extinguishers, and feverishly
cutting away metal, what can stick
in the craw, what sobers, shocks, bewilders,
is that swinging guarantor of luck:
St. Christopher, the Christ-child on his shoulders.

# Christ of the Deep

*A large replica of Guido Galletti's religious sculpture
is sited in twenty-one feet of water off Key Largo.*

Grouper nose me.
Striped bass make a pass,
a bombing run,
over my forehead.
Bonefish exhibit a certain curiosity.
That which I walked upon I stand under.
This baptism lasts forever.
The sea cries itself to sleep over
continental shelves, sloping shales.
Snorkelling evangelists love me.
Glass-bottomed boats leave me
gasping in their wake,
for this is Florida
and rubbernecks must return before
the happy hour.
Thank you, believers,
for such positioning;
yet the gesture lacked originality.
I am Christ the Copy.
The real me, my alter ego,
guards Old World waters off Genoa.
Here my disciples are snook and flounder,
pompano and bluefish.
Like the shark I never sleep.
My arms are raised eternally
in a hopeless gesture of forgiveness,
a drowned futility relevant only to the likes
of this black mullet which,
like Judas,
mouths my cheek.

## Nessiteras Rhombopteryx

Sonar equipment. An American gay
with big money and a handlebar
moustache. And always the mountains
not listening, wool gathering, heads
in a mist. Ryan has been loading his nostrils
freely. The boat rocks
itself to sleep; water cradles it,
grey and cold as a New York dawn.
"The mother's down there somewhere."
A grin shows discoloured teeth. The tattoo
is of a virgin ravished by a snake.
Tyler has come-to-bed eyes. Bleary
with desire, he tunes in on expensive
equipment. Scotland is a drag;
but next week he will be in Amsterdam
where the real action is. "Locate
and kill," Ryan says when questioned.
"There's no other way." Single malt
for breakfast. The Fort William lad wonders
where the girls are. Discoloured teeth again.
A Loch Ness Monster? There are two:
one from Queens, the second from L.A.
Clouds chase each other across the speeded-
up sky. Weird psychosexual behaviour.

# The Inner Sound

Here, between Applecross Bay and Raasay, lies
the Inner Sound. You can hear it
when all else is quiet, when gulls and humans
have been stilled by darkness. It is
the holding of breath before a wave breaks,
before another gust buffets your cheek.
Long ago, Maelrubha built a monastery nearby
to tap into the inner sound of peace.
Miraculously thirteen hundred years
are held in the palm of my hand, scooped
from the brine which spills in benediction
at my feet: centuries that are nothing
to the hermit crab, so monklike within
its twist of shell, beside me on the sand.
Strange how the seconds seem long and awful,
as if we are waiting, as if this hunger
cannot be assuaged. Normality is restored
by the small red boat which chugs
towards Eilean Mór, the largest of the Crowlins,
islands which haunt my southern side.
Willy Ross, for he is the owner,
ignores – or does not see – my wave.
He is too busy thinking of pollack
and whiting, as are the scavengers
swooning like bridesmaids about his wake.
How odd that, though I love the silence here,
I find that motor's throb more comforting.

# Just Fancy

The anecdote, bizarre and bold, seems Dylan's final antic:
his coffin in a cargo hold over the Atlantic,
and on it sailors playing cards, pale and bleary-eyed,
unobservant of the bard's cadaver inside.
The aeroplane, the endless waves, the feisty game of poker...
Dylan is the pawky knave, jack-the-lad, and joker.

Down below the polished lid now and ever after
sense the poet bet a quid, hear the puckish laughter.
Dylan, flying home to Wales, spins his final yarn,
tells the tallest of his tales. Soon the soil of Laugharne
will bring its own distinguished rain drumming on the wood.
Now coarse fingers cross the grain in light-hearted mood.

Ace and king and queen descend. Sailors take their sport.
Caitlin won't accept the end. Frantic, overwrought,
she paces through a haze of doubt; her husband takes his ease.
He does not hear her wail and shout. Death's *cheval-de-frise*
hedges him about. He's cold, yet still the old romantic:
Dylan in a cargo hold crossing the Atlantic.

# Lost Cause

"Two-thirds of the world is covered by water," we said,
'you don't need a bicycle." Still she looked dubious.
There is no convincing some fish. "Swim," we urged,
"claim your birthright." However, all she thought about
were saddles and handlebars. "Go as far and as deep
as you want. Men these days are effectively surplus
to requirements. The seas have been liberated
as never before." Yet she was asking about panniers
and a hand pump. Next she would be stipulating a
                                        headlamp
and her very own cycle lane. "Women are free now,"
we cried. "Why do you still want to be enslaved?"
But she had the eyes of a dead haddock, and her mouth
hung open as if hungry for bait, and she turned
against the tide of history and the current of advice
and transformed herself into an animated Magritte.
The last we saw of her she was peddling
lugubriously inland, wobbling off to her doom,
her conditioned requirement, her phallus-bearer.

# The Trier

She's been to Totleigh Barton and Lumb Bank
        and somewhere else in Wales
and has been brought by tutors to the brink

of Real Poetry. It's like Real Ale,
        something good and true,
yet progress seems outpaced by every snail.

She's bought the books and even read them too.
        She's got the autographs
on flyleaves. But she still cannot break through

to personal greatness. So she writes for laughs
        and friends and bottom drawers,
seeking inspiration in carafes

increasingly. When poets get applause
        she dies a little. How
by following the same stylistic laws

does she fail to build her wall, or plough
        her furrow? Where's the lack?
She even slept with someone great in Slough –

well, almost great, though afterwards felt slack
        rather than elated.
Her words are polished and her humour's black,

her turn of phrase is witty and not dated,
        yet editors turn her down –
or not her but the gems she has created.

Perhaps one day she'll wear the poet's crown
        and not feel stale or droopy.
Perhaps one day she'll woo them up in town

and be more than a branch official (NUPE).
    Until then she will be
an also-ran, a literary groupie.

# The Poetry Pool

As ever, the young ones want to make a splash.
Their elders and betters have seen it all before:
carefree run, intimidating bombshell of freak publicity,
choppy waves. Several veterans hope the exhibitionists
will disappear without trace. In the roped-off section
mellow lady poets swim up and down, hoping to maintain
their sales figures, their tight tummies. They studiously ignore
the parvenus. The Scots have arrived, and make a rumpus
at the shallow end, shouting to each other in Lallans;
while in the deep end the odd don floats and murmurs,
fondly remembering when Leavis swam the Channel
heroically. In changing cubicles a few hesitant poetasters
flex muscles, pull on trunks, and wonder whether
the cool water will enlarge or diminish their manhood.
The Caribbean lifeguard raps solipsistically;
from his vantage point he assumes some sort of superiority.
No one's drowned here for years, though many
have emerged shrivelled, depleted, not having fulfilled
early promise. The worst thing is the voices.
They never stop. Bright, shrill, self-referential, they rise
to the high ceiling, expand to the wide walls,
and rarely doubt their stature, their prowess.

# The Last Resort

Tom Stack and I sat outside The Last Resort, clutching
cracked tankards. The foul brew was better than nothing.
He was a cutpurse and highwayman, gibbeted
in 1740. I was pressed from a later vintage
of sour grapes. A Brueghel peasant flopped past
on crutches, rotten teeth set in a grin of effort.
Two dogs were humping with hollow expressions beside
a milestone. "I come straight here," he said.
"The rope, then this. It's no England I recognise,
yet much seems familiar." I couldn't help but agree.
It was a village idyll with the juice of comfort
drained away, the marrow of reassurance picked out.
And why did it stay a summer's evening just before thunder?
The air never ceased to be oppressive. The rusty sign
creaked in the breeze. There was otherwise silence,
apart from the moaning of an old woman (who'd been dying
for months, years some said) in an upstairs room.
Her daughter brought her a bucket of cinders to eat.
This elicited scant response. "Why you here?"
enquired Stack, his words edged with indifference.
"Poetry", I said. "What thee mean?" he continued.
"I kept writing it. My family went without, the poor
were not relieved, great causes remained unchampioned.
This is my reward." Already he had stopped listening.
A horse and cart carrying faggots groaned into view.
The tired driver asked where the fire was.
"In the quarry beyond the hill," grunted Tom Stack.
We watched the ancient beast plod wearily on.

# Incommunicado

What sort of a marriage is this? She hasn't
spoken to me all day. I've started to blame myself:
something I've said must be responsible for
those tears. And when I speak she doesn't answer;
she just looks disconsolate. Her behaviour
is atypical, hard to fathom; for years
we've got on well, with few disputes. Then this.
And why does she put our displayed photographs
in a drawer, prepare lunch only for herself, pick
at her food like a lovesick teenager? I try
to cheer her, but she's beyond reason, inarticulate,
inscrutable. This is ironic conduct for one
who spent time yesterday in church, though
what she was doing there – it being a Tuesday –
she has not said. "Look," I say, "be reasonable.
Tell me what's bothering you." But she rises, without
answering, and walks through me to the kitchen.

# Thomas William Ellis

The gravestone loses its words and returns to the quarry
where it was hewn. The ground in front of it bursts open
like a dropped egg; the coffin reappears for an instant
and is gone. An undertaker walks backwards to the slab
and draws the shroud down from the face, the face which
lies impassive beneath the distraught gaze of relatives
in a cramped bedroom. Their concern lessens, though only
slightly, as he opens his eyes; then night returns, followed
by the previous day and the night before that. He is
gathering pace. The rewind is faster than we can make
                                            sense of.
It is out of control seemingly, yet the chaos holds its own
internal order and meaning. Suddenly it stops the day before
the melanoma started, and we are in real time. He is moving
towards the moment the rogue cell began to multiply, and has
twenty-three hours to go. Perhaps, you hope, this time he can
do something, *anything*, to avoid a repetition. You lean
                                            forward,
tapping on the glass of the past, trying to attract
his attention, but he will have none of it. You hate the tune
he whistles, the way he screws the lid back on the pickle jar,
how he bends to stroke his dog, oblivious of the danger.

# Stranger in Town

Have you heard the way
he walks around the house?
Stiffly. His boots creak.
His leather pants are arthritic.
So much protection is at odds
with our suburban soft option,
our conventional semi.
He longs for the plains.
Why else would he be
so restless? His taciturnity
is becoming legendary. He picks
his teeth like a philosophy
of life. His eyes focus
horizons beyond our own.
Why doesn't he leave?
Why doesn't he ask for
money to buy a horse?
He could be happy
in Montana, Wyoming.
He could sit tall in the saddle,
in his element, allowing
his moodiness free rein.
What does he do here?
Nothing. We know better
than to patronise him with
country-and-western music,
pulp fiction set in Laramie,
videotaped cowboy films.
We've learned, almost,
to ignore him. Eventually
he'll come to his senses
and mooch off. Until then
we prepare his chow
and leave him to it.
Old brooder. Dark eyes.

# My Father, Shaving

This daily provision of feminine smoothness
seemed particularly masculine. It matched the way
a towel cleared a mirror's condensation.
He performed his toilet like Gary Cooper among
Oregon backwoods at dawn beside a lake;
it was as proud a ritual, despite our kitchen's banality.
The long-suffering sink accepted cream, brush, razor.
Propped on the windowsill, his reflection glowered.
He tilted forward, stripped to the waist,
concentration informing his features. Tightening
jowls with a forefinger, he drew blade across stubble,
avoiding the sacrosanct moustache. He would hum:
not Sinatra or Crosby but Josef Locke. A styptic pencil
was seldom used. The marshal squatted to rinse
utensils in the shallows at his feet – just as an arrow
hit a tree mere feet away. He reflexively
reached for his revolver in its ornate holster.
My father turned simultaneously towards
the whistle of the kettle, and, grace under fire,
switched off the gas with cool aplomb.
It would be a newer vision of her husband
that brought my mother a Coronation mug of tea.
His cheeks would shine like china.

# Late Discovery

The General Register Office, asked
to find my parents' marriage date,
say nothing can be found between
nineteen forty-one and -five
(the target years). What is unmasked
is their robust cohabitation;
meanwhile, from this morning, I've
become an illegitimate.

Both are dead; and no one cares
about their history but me.
Conjugal pretence suited them
no doubt. Their 18-carat rings
signified that pact of theirs
was evidence of bride and groom,
the bond of commoners and kings
and not the tilth of bastardy.

# Helvellyn Incident, 1805

The rocks were terrible cushions. The sky turned
from noon to midnight. Days multiplied like
a hall of mirrors. Mr. Gough's terrier pined,
limbs increasingly prominent, flesh thinning
over rib vaults. Her master changed incomprehensibly:
his skin became soapy, his wounds fungal; his body
renounced its reassuring smells of eau de Cologne
and tobacco. The animal waited patiently beside
the rancid conundrum which had coddled and fed it.
Some weeks later both were found, as were
the smashed easel's geometries, the palette's
rigidity, paint blocks strewn like small change.
The gentleman artist was finally buried,
his faithful companion a leashed mourner.
The materials were carefully assembled, exhibits
at a trial where circumstance alone stood in the dock.
Onlookers solemnly observed the pristine pencils,
the unused sable brushes, the innocent colours
still in their wrappers awaiting their owner's touch.

# Fabulist

Nice one, Aesop, though it didn't save you
being flung over a cliff in your fifty-sixth year.
Your body went down in geography, just as
your name went down in history. Splash or crunch,
the outcome was the same. Had you been less sardonic
you would have lasted longer as a man
yet shorter as an icon of early wit,
pre-Christian parable, and cracker-barrel philosophy.
There you are, in mid-air, your murderers
looking on gleefully as you head for oblivion,
but let us freeze the frame. About you
foxes and grapes, geese and golden eggs,
jackdaws, monkeys, and peacocks bloom,
a cornucopia of characters caught
in a modest rainbow between hate and death.
Suddenly you, a deformed Phrygian slave
who went one aphorism too far, are invulnerable,
surrounded forever by your colourful creations.
My finger hovers above the button.

# Alma Mater

Fights were frequent and bloody. There was
a war going on, though mostly a cease-fire ruled.
Without warning, hostilities would recommence,
not among groups, between individuals. The cause
was less antipathy than the underscoring
of pecking orders. Never since have I seen
teeth coughed out, or a victim reel from a punch
as if falling backwards a second into the past.
Uniforms and boaters provided a veneer of propriety;
vol-au-vents and petits fours in Speech Day marquees
made staff the equal of minor royalty;
oils and honours boards in the wainscoted hall
reminded us that excellence was pursued here.
How strangely and strongly this was offset
by the bespectacled fat boy held by his ankles
from a second-floor window, raining pens
and predecimal coinage from flapless pockets.

# The Experiment

The biblical chocolates seemed a good idea.
They kept the Brothers busy and the boys happy,
blending originality and hedonism, producing a flagellation
only the walnuts felt in their hard brown spirals.
The Trinity in Neapolitan nougat. A pistachio John the Baptist.
Wild berry Gospels. How we would love religion after this!
But was it possible to get pi-jaw from toffee?
And would the difference between duty and gratification
appear a fudge? The headmaster decreed less sweetness.
Matron concurred: the spotless were getting spotty.
Yet we still had Christian Union next to the tuck shop.
The chaplain still sprinkled us with a vermicelli blessing.
Dissenters arose, pupils who recognised the gimmick for
                                              what it was.
Belief, they insisted, should not be marshmallow;
it should resemble Christ's forty days without confectionery,
tramping the Wilderness, resisting temptation –
the saccharine blandishments of the Great Seducer.
A backlash formed. Chapel was suddenly sugar-free.
We began to exult in its plainness, even its sourness.
The Brothers were worried. Their vats slipped into torpor;
their stirring exploits, their sexy additives,
were becoming history. We filed, seraphic choristers,
from the vestry, heads held high and hymnals in place,
towards the waiting stalls, knowing that Turkish delight
was for Mussulmans, acid drops for wimps.
We'd seen through our educators' stratagems
and weren't as gullible as they'd imagined.
The headmaster, in his special pew, was po-faced,
eyes glistening with something other than radiance.

# The Farmer's Wife and her Brood

*A whistling woman and a crowing hen*
*are neither fit for God nor men.*
Scottish proverb

Chickens made the best worshippers. They clucked
and squawked, had a diocesan pecking order,
and revered the episcopal cock in his blatant finery.
They were noisy in their denunciation of anything
which did not accord with their creed; and walked
awkwardly, with fat feathered thighs, as though laden
with bric-a-brac for a fête. They had
a Sunday school for chicks, and should each Easter
have celebrated by distributing chocolate human embryos.
Because all groups must, for solidarity, demonise somebody,
Satan had a brush and pointed nose, sharp ears
and keen eyes. Hell was in the earth, feeding
voracious cubs. His wicked wife was a wanton vixen
whose wild cries during oestrus rang through
the coniferous plantation like the calls of the damned.
But so long as the worshippers congregated in their church
of chipboard and wire netting, evil could be kept at bay.
I ended up not knowing whether I preferred the fox
or the hens. Their fussy sanctimoniousness often
stuck in my gullet: they were too sure of themselves
by half, as was their stout, no-nonsense owner
who crossed the field carrying a grain bucket
at the same time every day, venting the same
high-pitched tune, lips puckered like an ovipositor.

# Life: Made in Taiwan

Assemble. You will see the bits.
When they fit, baby will come after
though down the line. Keep it clean,
keep it warm; keep it refrigeration
of food. Watching it grow ever
and stronger son, or having daughter.
When it schooling make it violin:
this will be big bucks in adult showcase
with luckspin. Television with care.
Junk will be frowned. Our Company say
education: locksmith, animal clinic,
pearl high-tech with boats. Film,
as it (boy, girl) soon not young either
but American teenage type. Say
gum banned. Walking tall better.
Say about shoulders, and strong teeth.
We say fish because longevity.
All exam hardness good for bucks,
so our advice keen. Avoid horses.
Avoid old way, but gods good.
Wear glasses for clearer eyes.
Sport. American basketball. Dating
agency better than persons on corridor
or other floor. We say chromosomes
and blood test. Hard work mostly.
Components assembly and big toy.
Evenings saké and putting in laughter.
Courtship with cosmetic (Company
will advise askers: please ask).
Courtesy like parents. Virgin like parents
until multiplying marriage on Astroturf
with many thousand bride and groom.
Indoor climate and dome. No rain
on veil. We advise honeymoon night
only, with work prompt soon.

Assemble. You will see the bits.
When they fit, baby will come after
though down the line. Keep it clean,
keep it warm; keep it refrigeration.

# Polaroid: Chandpur

The welfare worker takes a photograph.
The camera sticks out its tongue,
on which, melting into life
like a communion wafer, Anwar forms
– proud, a beggar, standing by his wife,
worn, exhausted, relatively young,
yet able still to bare his teeth and laugh.
The sun is high. Dust and flies, in swarms,

fill the air or settle. Soon she will
bring another baby into grief.
The welfare worker hands the photograph
to Anwar. He treasures it. A death
might be better. Leaning on his staff,
dressed in rags, frail as a fallen leaf,
he avidly awaits the beautiful
agony, the bloodshed, the first breath.

# In the Kabul McDonald's

That a medium Chicken McNuggets contains eight grams
of saturated fat per portion Kim found acceptable.
The Khyber Pass had left her peckish. I placed
my Indiana Jones safari hat on the melamine tabletop.
Others eyed us warily, though my partner's voraciousness
was a source of amusement: a Western white woman
with bare arms and braceleted wrists devouring without
a hint of European sophistication. The left trouserleg
of the heavy-browed tribesman at the next table
flapped from the knee. Although most locals understood
only Dari or Pushtu, she and I never openly discussed
politics or religion. The jihad was still a dangerous rumour
among local thoroughfares. He leant across: "Chicken good.
So Hash Brown and Sundae Caramel Topping."
His suspicious eyes were otherwise inscrutable,
yet the crow's-feet of the high plains denizen
threatened mirth at any moment. Kim helpfully responded:
"Hash browns have only half carbohydrates of ice cream,
so healthier." The tribesman frowned and reached for
his home-made rifle, a cumbersome artefact not unlike
an arquebus. The small hairs at my nape rose.
He swivelled it towards us with surprising ease.
"But carbohydrates great," Kim said with a quickness
which imperilled pronunciation, "unless you overweight,
which you not." He offered the monstrosity to us
with proprietorial pride. "McNuggets good. Gun good,"
he beamed. We forgave his unclassifiable breath
and imperfect dentition. Kim went to touch the weapon
as expected, but turned her action into a delicate wave.
He tucked the loose trouserleg under his thigh
and turned to his Quarter Pounder with evident relish.

# Overlooked

(Andreas Mihavecz, Bregenz)

Forgotten by the police for eighteen days
in a holding cell in Höchst, Austria,
he dreams now of locked doors
most nights, the key in Australia,

at the ocean floor, on the moon.
No food or water passed his lips until,
near death, he was found by someone.
Imagine the apologies, the Get Well

card from the Polizeipräsident. "Sorry.
It won't happen again. You're unique!"
Andreas puts it aside, smiles wanly,
feels the shadow lessening in each cheek,

under his eyes, his xylophonic ribs
which Trudi photographed to forestall the crime
of cover-up. 'That hideous job's
taken him away too long this time'

she'd thought, and cursed him for not phoning.
Meanwhile, his cries of protest went unheard;
only the brickwork knew of his complaining,
and it wasn't saying a word.

# Homunculus

I am the dwarf; but what is more terrible
than my grin is my raincoat. My eyes
are silverfish darting. Watch them
for an inkling of enchantment. My skin
is that of a night watchman, a twentieth-
century troglodyte, tanned only by
the neon of clubland. You said you knew
about Vienna, could take the city in your stride;
but some streets sent you reeling, your high heels
mocked by the cobbles. So you were reduced
to hurrying down the pavement in your tights.
That's when it began to rain. I stepped
out of a doorway, from my cobweb of shadows;
and you, a hesitant fly, not fearing a dwarf
half as much as the shower's dishevelment,
accepted my suggestion: a drink, your fortune told,
and no names traded. Now you walk
my treadmill. The iron grating ten metres above
crosshatches your cage with intimations
of lost freedoms. I want no more
than your cold presence among these depths,
these vaulted caverns that are half my world,
a never-ending antidote to Strauss,
your life the flywheel in my clockwork house.

# Hans Werner Schneider, 22 May 1942

He is thinking of the Bugatti his late brother raced,
though here there are no roads, only invisible bends
where gulls perform slick turns. North Rona extends
about him, the last place on earth. His map shows
the nearest land, forty miles away: the Butt of Lewis.
Somewhere *der Führer* rants, but all that is heard
are persistent birds, freewheeling with cries
of derision. No one would have seen him crash-land.
He has become a nonperson. There is no escape.
'The island of seals' will be his graveyard.
Yet he can smell engine oil and see Günter
tinkering with the supercharger in their bright garage
on this, Wagner's birthday. Within the shelter
of a dry-stone croft, abandoned last century, he sits
in full uniform on the only furniture, a kitchen chair,
as sturdy now as when last used. His compass
shows where Mainz should be. He faces it,
and glimpses – beyond stout walls and grey waves –
the towns of the Prussian Rhine. As he unscrews
his cyanide phial, a whiff of bitter almonds greets him.
No caring nurse stands near with stomach pump,
respirator, syringe of sodium thiosulphate.
He lifts it to his lips. Family gather at the open door
and two gaping windows: Mother, both nieces,
two uncles, and the Lutheran pastor allowing
that, under the circumstances, suicide is not a sin.

# Otto von Bismarck, 1870

Never were walrus moustache and spiked helmet
more caricatural. He was what he wore.
Polished epaulettes, stiff collar,
Gilbertian military mien: the man was a joke
but no joke. The power, not to be trifled with,
represented a society in no mood
for the small gesture. He was the mask,
and the mask glittered with uneasy strength –
the formality of boots yet to be broken in,
a whip yet to be used in anger
or exhortation. His eye focused as coldly
as that of any damned Englishman. His blood
travelled soundlessly along veins
of quite exceptional Teutonic plumbing.
And his breath smelt of the deaths
of the nonexistent, the yet-to-be-conceived.

# The Father of Danish Astronomy

Tycho Brahe had a golden nose,
which sounds as nice as nasty
things can get. Sixteenth-century rhinoplasty

was brave yet crude. He sat
at night stargazing, where no one could see
his noble deformity:

an amber proboscis
that was worth
its weight, and yet he'd gladly give the earth

to repossess the heavenly body of
a natural protuberance. Thus fate
kept him up late

and, while the world worked,
took him to his bed
on whose pillow one astounding head

would sleep the day away, dreaming
of planetary motions beyond number,
the choreography of gilded slumber.

# The Exception and The Rule

*The Duke of Wellington opposed railways*
*"because they would encourage the lower classes to move about".*

A ped of biddies tumbles from a lap, squawking, clucking.
An unkempt moiler shambles aboard, clutching a blackjack
of swipes. Three ragged bantlings snivel contemptuously
as their mother pours vituperation over them.
A ganger in caked gaiters and encrusted sabots
sits nearby, hollow cheeks underscoring
                                    a consumptive cough
(he frequently holds a rag to pallid lips).
Commotion, stench, and never enough room!
Bedford starts to slide backwards.
The morning begins. The great unwashed are on the move.

The Iron Duke sybaritically applies
                        a warm towel to his cheeks,
eyes the gilt-framed mirror, smiles. A servitor nods,
leaving the dressing room obsequiously.
                            Today it will be bezique,
billiards, croquet, a perambulation with the mastiffs
about the grounds of Apsley House, postprandial repose,
and thanks to God for all this benison.

# The Spirit of Robin Hood

There was Steve, fresh from Durham Gaol, footloose
as any mercenary; Sharon, who craved excitement;
Griff, who'd dropped out of public school and society
years before; Al, who had a dragon on his buttocks
and a unicorn between his shoulder blades; and me.
Unfortunately, our victims played golf and bridge
with magistrates and circuit judges, which meant
natural justice got shafted. Yet it was good while it lasted:
car radios, televisions, mountain bikes, jewellery....
We flogged it, keeping a third of the proceeds
and giving the rest to local charities, who shamelessly
shopped us, having suspected we'd come by our moolah
illegally. For a while, though, it was walkways
through treetops, a Bedford van with flat tyres,
an encampment. We got put down for, apparently,
a fitting time. Process of law, they called it.
Retribution more like. But briefly we'd been
merry geezers, and Sharon had been a girl again,
tender as a shoot; and once, at night, we'd stopped,
tilted our ears to the breeze, and heard the shouts
of zealous adventurers and thwarted pursuers,
and – high above the campfire – a shooting star
had pierced the velvet sky like a flaming arrow.

# The Proposal

At the dinner party, Nikolai
sounded drunk but was sober, such
were his landlocked vocables. Cubes
chinked in his Coke glass. His eyes
were meltwater in a face as red
as a gutted carp. He understood
I was 'in business': he too
was an (I helped him pronounce it)
'entrepreneur'. As I fondled
my brandy balloon in the lounge, he took
me aside. At Port Vladimir
lay a supernumerary icebreaker,
towable to Norway in the summer months,
at a knockdown price. Was I interested?
Our host's diamond necklace glinted
wickedly. The drawing-room chandelier
hung its frozen branches, its bulbs
of dripping light. This was the thaw
the politicians had promised. "I might be,"
I lied; and Nikolai slapped my shoulder
with conviviality, his guttural laugh
as deep as permafrost, and radioactive.

# Omission Accomplished

*That's one small step for [a] man,*
*one giant leap for mankind.*
          Neil Armstrong: 21.7.69

Why, after years of general preparation, months
of detailed training, did he drop the indefinite article
where all the world was listening? It fell soundlessly
from his sentence, denting history as his feet
dented moondust. The impression lingers, unweathered,
unweatherable. Perhaps one should blame the emptiness
of the locale, the frozen heat of the moment, as he
jumped between known and unknown, a bear impersonating
a feather, and drifted off course into eleven-twelfths
of exactitude, the space between natural and supernal hands
on the Sistine Chapel ceiling. One supposes it could
have been worse: the voicing of virtual trash – *Tat's*
*one small step for a man* – in a definitive dropping of aitches.

# Three Devils

We were halfway through a marketing meeting when
a trio of large bats with malevolent human faces arrived
and climbed a wall to perch
                 – wings like half-closed umbrellas –
under a corner of the ceiling. They were
                         horned intelligentsia
on a dark mission. Their talk, when it came, was shrill
and condemnatory. We would have fled had they not
warned us against doing so. One of us, they proclaimed,
would be coming with them to infernal regions
within the hour; they wanted us to sweat first, to scour
consciences for evidence of malpractice so that
our candidacy would commend itself
                    and explain, if not excuse,
their presence. They said we could forego our own selection
if we nominated a scapegoat,
               one of our well-dressed number,
to carry our sins to the underworld. We decided
that casting lots was the fairest procedure. "Hurry!"
screeched one. "We cannot wait forever." Names
were written on identical cards, which were folded
and put in a drawer taken from the chairman's desk.
It was lifted above our heads, and Diane Smithers
was invited to stand on a chair and reach for one.
We were unimaginably tense. She handed it to
the team leader. He tentatively opened the card
and sighed with relief. "At least it isn't me," he said.

# Troglodytes, 1884

Here is the evidence: Great Britain
at the height of Empire, allowing
shellfish gatherers to live in a cave
near Seaton in Cornwall. They have
a strange appearance and a stranger tongue, being
Irish. Whether they speak Erse is uncertain.

There are three: a man and two women.
Their faces have integrity, a fierce
pride, as if to say *We are your equals*
*even though you treat us as insubstantial*
*scavengers. Our tears are your tears,*
*our joys your joys. We too are human.*

When they go to market via the Torpoint ferry
locals turn the other way. These are
raree-show oddities, hybrids, hardly
of the same species – yet hardy
enough, and skilled at bringing ashore
at low tide delicious crabs. We

owe them a debt of gratitude, but
it is far too late for the debt to be paid.
When the time came, priest and sexton
gave each an honest Christian
burial under some yew tree's shade.
Their cave has been empty for a century, shut

against the present, the inrush of progress,
though this photograph shows it with bodies
as alive as mine. I can see
strong folded arms, tidy
pinned-back hair, respectable bodice,
moleskin trousers, calico dress.

# Inspiration and Expiration

At the Henry Ford museum in Dearborn, Michigan
you will find, among other surprises,
not a reconstruction of Abe Lincoln's courthouse,
the Wright Brothers' cycle shop, and Edison's lab
but the real thing; and in that laboratory
you will discover not just what you would expect
in any such setting, but a vial said to contain
Edison's dying breath. You may not touch it,
but you can peer deeply past the glass into
the depths of that final exhalation, and wonder
about its predecessors – every one of them –
back to that first postnatal cry, and the doctor
peering over his steamed-up pince-nez at
the exhausted woman and saying, "Congratulations,
ma'am, we have ourselves a son." Tears
of relief commingled with pain came next,
and the new mother craned forward to see
the shadowiness that had for nine months
lived inside her. We can only speculate
upon her wish to observe more clearly
the living miracle she had produced, but no
light bulb existed yet for easy illumination.
Let us leave that room, for the corridor
beyond the door has amazingly transformed
itself to this same laboratory in New
Jersey thirty-two years later. The tiny fingers
and slimy little body you have just seen
are changed and tidy: a suit with waistcoat
and spotted neckerchief, and the inventor
converting sewing thread to carbon by baking it
for use as a filament. Soon this will
burn continuously for thirteen-and-a-half hours.
The laboratory is chill this October morning.
You can see Edison's breath on the air.

# According to the Statute Book

*When trains meet at a crossing both shall come to a full stop*
*and neither shall proceed until the other has gone.*

Kansas law

A woman could sort it out. The world's
most famous aviatrix came from just down
the road: this is Amelia Earhart country, though she
might have risen above it all, on wings
which sent a shadow scuttling across the prairie.
The hours are as inert as this rolling stock, which has
somewhere to go but little chance of getting there.
A wheel-tapper hawks and spits into the sand.
A uniformed inspector scratches his head
for the nth time; regulations state this
and nothing more – that institutionalised politeness
has precedence over timekeeping or even travel.
Stasis smells like steam and engine oil;
it geysers forth or drips onto the track.
Wichita by sundown is unlikely. The municipality
becomes more of an abstract noun by the minute.
A philosophy professor bound for Oklahoma City
checks his watch; his lecture on Will Power
will not get delivered. Through the carriage window
he eyes the endless wheat. He was brought up
out here, but it was never as still as this then.
He recognises the variety: Turkey Red,
a hardy winter strain, brought over
from Russia in 1874 by Mennonite settlers.
The youth opposite is prepared
for a long wait; he slips Michael Jackson
into his Discman yet again, and adjusts
his headphones. A young girl scampers
down the aisle wearing washable colours

on cheeks and forehead, a white
Native American. Does she know,
wonders the delayed speaker, that Wichita
in the local Indian language means 'painted faces'?

# Wowsers

Mrs. Simpson Aggregate was a wowser,
breast-fed her daughter,
went with a neighbour
to Longreach for

supplies every fortnight.
They prayed together.
Averted their sight
at each male encounter

in shop or street.
Mrs. Anelie Barraquat
weathered the heat,
though Mrs. Simpson Aggregate

cursed its devil presence,
hated its beads of sweat.
The two ladies never once
spoke to each other: that

kept the pressure at intense
levels, a boil they would lance
only when returning. At a safe distance
from the town, they dismantled their defence

mechanisms and let smiles dance.
Several hours later, back
on the farm, they opened the dense
Bible and read until dark.

Queensland cooled itself with the lick
of night. Against their rocking-chairs' creak,
Simpson and Anelie would talk
on the veranda. One would give suck.

And a million stars would wink
at their relationship,
so effortlessly in sync.
And the child would sleep.

# Bridges

Always they remain faithful,
like tethered animals waiting to bear
our bulk, which they do uncomplainingly.
Science demonstrates that the purest
aesthetically are also the most efficient
in terms of construction and maintenance.
They are faith writ large, a quantum leap
into the future, a demonstration
of man's capacity to humble abysses,
to cock a snook at torrents.
It is as if we took God on
in the matter of rainbows.

Our hands were a bridge. You and I
were linked by strands stronger than steel.
Nothing hinted at shifting foundations.
No one glimpsed the metal fatigue.
All the world saw were girders,
cables, reinforced concrete, smiles.
Adultery was a light aircraft
crashing into one of the pillars.

# Chicken Kiev for One

She bends above the shining foil
– St. Sophia's under snow
lit by moonlight or the glow
of a Ukrainian afternoon
in winter. Thoughts do not defile
her actions, though they may do soon.

She rolls the breast in grated cheese,
parsley and pepper. Seasoned flour
coats it. A clock tells the hour
on Kreshchatik, Kiev's main street.
"I'll do exactly as I please.
To eat alone is still to eat.

He could not stop me being me."
She beats the brains out of an egg,
adds water, breadcrumbs. Life is big
and she is small. Her fingers waltz.
She hums. She smiles beatifically.
The *matryoshkas* (Russian dolls)

she bought at the Intourist shop
watch calmly from the windowsill.
If thoughts could injure, hers would kill.
But why let bitter memories spoil
delicious food? She bids them stop.
The chicken sinks through sizzling oil.

# Imaginary Intervention

I am stepping back a decade into this school photograph
from which my five-year-old beams. Each settled infant
wonders why I have appeared, as do their posing teachers.
I flutter fingers at them, and walk to the nearest phone box.
Ten minutes later a taxi draws up. "Where to, squire?"
I name your village. He nods: "I know the one;
about fifteen miles...." Within half an hour I am paying him
and striding up your drive. You do not know me yet.
We will not formally meet for nine more years.
"Listen, I have news from the future about your husband.
He is going to leave you high and dry. He will break your heart.
Already I can name the other woman. I can give you chapter
and verse." But you believe none of it; naturally I am
'seriously disturbed'. Minor prophets have no place
in today's world. Worried and scared, you say in an undertone:
"I think you had better leave. I'm not sure what your game is
but unless you go now I shall be forced to call the police."
Disappointed, yet not surprised, I turn and depart. That night
he enters you with the same delicate passion you have known
since the courtship during which you both lost your virginity.
You ponder, even at the height of love, whether the stranger
had some purchase on the truth, but force it from your mind
as he explosively reassures you that no one could ever
take your place beneath his glowing weight.

# Mrs.

Three letters, two syllables, one badge
worn invisibly on the chest, as if to say
I'm Annexed. Please Redirect That Urge
Elsewhere. I uneasily

look at the married woman, take her in;
only that glint of gold at a finger hints
at appropriation. An unseen man
stands at her shoulder. He fishes, hunts,

and picks berries with her. I cannot.
He'd club me to a pulp if I darkened
the threshold to his cave, his moated fort,
his ranch-style bungalow. He'd call me friend

over a round of golf, a glass of beer,
but this lithe creature remains out of bounds.
Mrs. You're spoken for. You house my fear
and lust. Your pulchritude astounds.

# The Orthodox Chapel of St. Dyfrig

is down a lane in a quiet
private garden (quite
a surprise). Several steps. A door.
Beyond, you suddenly see a painted rood
screen and, bright as new coins,
numerous icons.
Sit on one of the two
benches. Having a child in tow
is no problem. Saints
glow like expensive satin;
daylight is lanced
by a lighted candle.
Already you will glimpse the priest.
If clothes were fruits, the ripest
would be found here. He presides
in vestments which only a despiser
of opulence would fault. The altar's
divine yet worldly, astral
and terrestrial in one. Notes
rise from the cantors, tones
which sweetly enhance these
proceedings via printed sheet
and clear voice. Observe.
There is nothing otiose or verbose:
everything is calm and sober.
Complementing the robes
exquisitely, the niceness
of various incenses
pervades the ritual. There
is a sense of celestial ether
in this assemblage, of others
elsewhere, among the throes
of religious observance in a far
country. The brush of Fra
Filippo Lippi could not have produced decor
more befitting a credo.

These days, when spiritual crusades
are less popular than used cars,
when in many countries
the pace is set by the cretinous
and traditional religion declines
until it is almost silenced,
how refreshing to see the earnest
antiquity of the Eastern
Church. Watch it glisten!
Marvel as your flesh tingles.
Here there are no gnomic
utterances about the Second Coming,
nothing stateside and Episcopal
underwritten by Pepsi-Cola;
here the blessing
has no commercial glibness
but a straight and simple
honesty which impels
belief. The nastily
second-rate shrinks beside saintly
composure, not grandiose
but unobtrusively organised
to allow the soul deepest
reverence, steeped
in timelessness. The mood
is not one of doom
but of immaculate strength. Outside
the world maintains its tedious
pattern of persistent
greed. Inside, prettiness
and purity obtain, priestly
solemnity balanced by spritely
youngsters with fresh faces.
Forget the press of cafés
and shops, hotel suites
with their passionate silhouettes,

casinos and racetracks where hedonists
engage in the nearly dishonest.
Sometimes the world can of itself
virtually stifle
the human spirit. Here, Mary
and Child are stronger than an army
yet meeker than the dew
which exists to wed
the grass. Maddening
profit motive and demanding
deadline slacken to the gentler paces
of the stars in space
in a place such as this.
Patience hits
its target, where the docile
moment lies innocently coiled.
Egotism and the flesh
are put aside on a shelf
until later; we are ageless for a time
as the sacred words emit
their essence. Angst
shrinks to the proportion of gnats;
the atheist and agnostic
are benightedly coasting
to their predictable end,
like a sick lion to its den.
The clowns, the morose
unassuageable Romeos,
the agitators, the muddled clerics
who in useless circles
have for too long gyrated,
all agents of tragedy
are elsewhere. Here the unaltering
Trinitarian triangle
outwits the damned, the Dantean,
the mind at an end.

It outshines the insatiable
appetites, the banalities,
the intrigues of boardroom and bedroom
that too often lead to boredom.
Here the only couples
observed in close-up
have heads bowed in a mildness
which is very far from mindless.
The future may be nuclear,
overcrowded, unclear,
but for now stillness reigns
until, softly, a singer
continues the praise
to which humble hearts aspire.
And when we are gaoled
in a questionable old age,
we shall remember being
where all true hopes begin:
with prayer and praise and psalm
lit by golden lamps.

## Acknowledgements

All the poems in this collection have previously been published. Several have won prizes in open competition.

Acknowledgements are due to:

*Ambit, Bête Noire, Bournemouth Festival Anthology, Critical Survey, Encounter, Envoi, Exeter Poetry Prize Anthology, Expansions, Unlimited, Leicester Poetry Society Anthology, London Magazine, Mallard Anthology, New Forest Poetry Society Anthology, New Welsh Review, Oxford Quarterly Review, Poetry from Aberystwyth IX and X, Poetry Nottingham, Poetry Review, Poetry Society Limited Edition Anthology, Poetry Wales, Ripley Competition Anthology, Smiths Knoll, Sourozh, Stand, Swagmag, Swanage Arts Festival Anthology, Tabla, Tees Valley Writer, The Frogmore Papers, The Swansea Review, The Times Literary Supplement, Thumbscrew, The Western Mail.*